For Daniel Eli and all the children of future generations. To Uncle Isaac, without you, this story would not be possible. To the Woodard/Woodward family and descendants. We will continue the fight for justice and equality because Black Lives will always Matter.

COPYRIGHT @2020 Laura M. Williams
All rights reserved. No part of this publication may be reproduced, distributed or transmitted in any form or by any means, including photocopying, recording, electronic or mechanical methods without prior written communication from the author, except in the case of brief quotations embodied in critical reviews and certain other non-commercial uses permitted by copyright law. For permission requests, send an email to TheBlindingofIsaacWoodard@gmail.com.

ISBN- 978-1-7356842-0-8 (Hardcover)
ISBN- 978-1-7356842-1-5 (Paperback)
ISBN- 978-1-7356842-2-2 (eBook)

First printing edition 2020

The descendants of Sgt. Isaac Woodard, Jr. honor his legacy by sharing his story, in his voice, through a children's book. The book is based on a true story of a forgotten decorated African-American Hero, on the fateful day of February 12, 1946, when a trip home changed America forever.

I am Sergeant Isaac Woodard, Jr., you probably won't find my name in the textbooks, so I'm going to tell you my story. I was born on March 8, 1919, in Winnsboro, South Carolina.

I grew up on a farm and life was really difficult. My father was a sharecropper. He grew cotton, corn, and other crops that he had to share with the white landowner.

My grandfather's name was Alex Woodard. He was born in 1843 and lived to be 108 years old. My grandpa, Alex, was enslaved and brought to America illegally from the Igbo Tribe in Nigeria, West Africa.

When I became a young man, I enlisted in the Army and then traveled overseas. During World War II, I proudly served my country, earned medals, and was promoted to Sergeant.

On February 12, 1946, I took the Greyhound Bus home. I asked the bus driver, during a rest stop, to allow me to use the restroom. The white bus driver spoke to me disrespectfully. I stood up to him. I told him to treat me like a man, the same way I treated him. Back then, a lot of white people didn't like Black people and they didn't treat us fairly. He became angry then called the police on me. Police Officer, Lynwood Shull, showed up and beat me and blinded me. That was the last day I ever saw daylight.

After the incident, life was difficult. My parents, brothers, sisters and other relatives took good care of me. I am so grateful for my family.

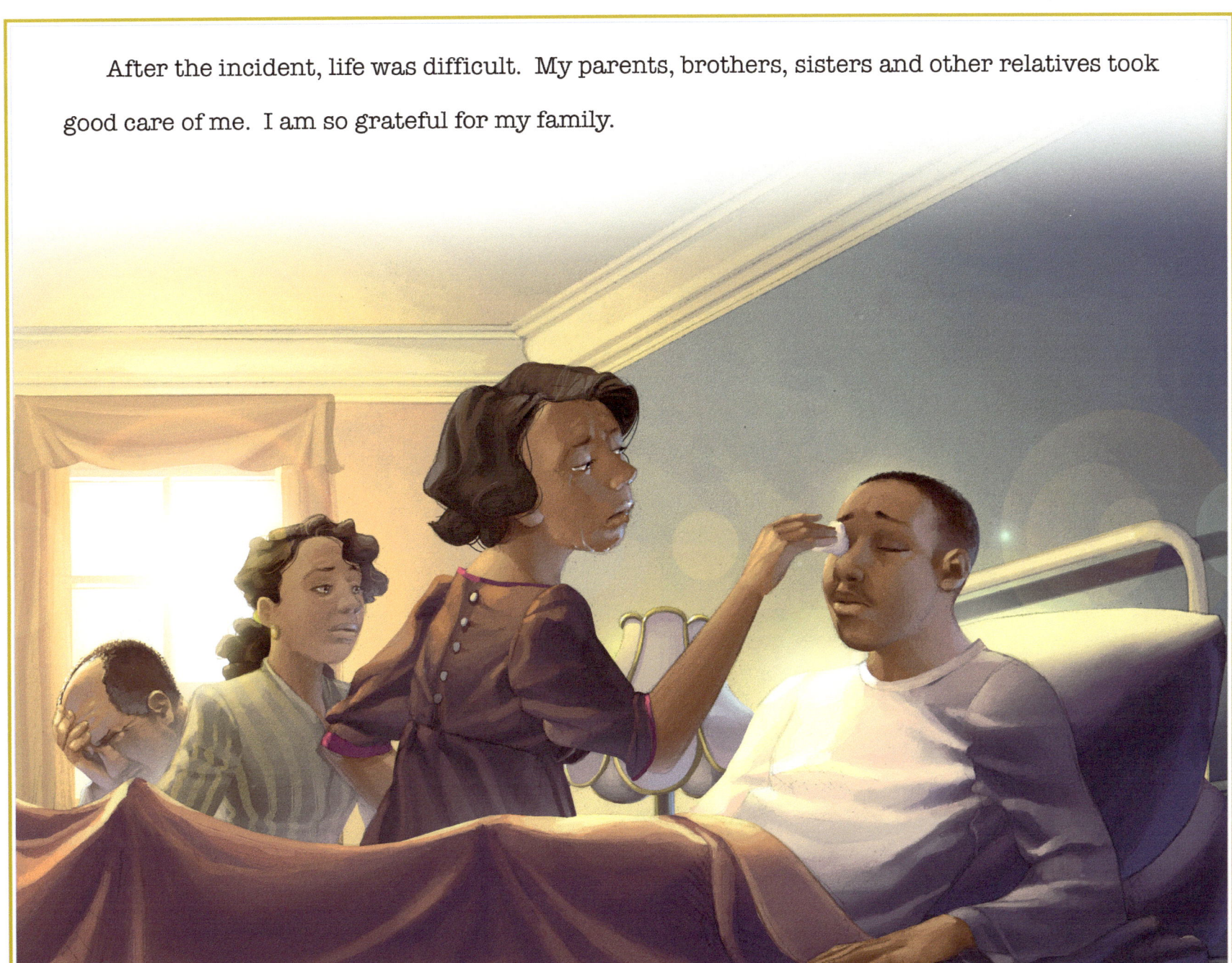

Many people were outraged by what happened to me and they showed their support. News spread quickly around the country, then around the world. Both Black and white people came together to change how Black people were being treated. Soon after, the beginning of the Civil Rights movement started in America.

People from all over the world wrote me letters of encouragement. One day, I received a letter from a little girl in Germany who heard about my story and she wanted to help. She sent me her $8 savings.

Everyone knew me as "The Blind GI" because that was what they called soldiers back then. The NAACP - The National Association for the Advancement of Colored People helped me too. They organized a music concert for me and entertainers like Nat King Cole, Billie Holiday, Pearl Bailey, Count Basie, and Boxer Joe Louis were in attendance to help raise funds. All the tickets sold out in one day.

I began a speaking tour and spoke to people all over the country to help stop injustices against Black people in America.

It was hard for Black people back then. Jim Crow laws in the South made it legal to segregate Black people. We were not allowed to eat in restaurants, or drink from the same water fountain, or use the same bathroom as white people. There were "White Only" and "Colored" signs.

President Harry S. Truman heard about my story and it made him sad. He knew he had to do something to make a change. So, he put together a Council on Civil Rights and changed the law and removed segregation from the Armed forces in 1948. Black and white soldiers were able to fight in the war side-by-side.

Judge J. Waites also changed laws. In 1951, he removed segregation in the schools and all the children, both Black and white, were able to go to school together. But a lot of white people did not like the change.

Rosa Parks

Dr. Martin Luther King

If you ever heard of Rosa Parks, Dr. Martin Luther King, or Malcolm X, you now know that I was part of history, too. Some desegregation laws also changed because of my story.

Malcolm X

Sgt. Isaac Woodard, Jr.

I am grateful for all the people who showed compassion, lifted my spirits, and contributed to the change of racial prejudice toward African-Americans. It made me feel really good to see Black and white people come together to stop the mistreatment of Black people and stand up against police brutality in America. Together, we can make it a great country for all of us.

What followed is an incredible story of angst, courage and motivation on behalf of Sgt. Woodard, President Harry S. Truman and Judge J. Waites Waring. This incident contributed to The Civil Rights Movement and quickly gained momentum.

Sgt. Woodard becomes a griot and unravels his story in simplistic form for the child reader to grasp an unforgiving, yet necessary part of history, while sparing them the story's horrific details. Sgt. Woodard illuminates the history of inequality for African-Americans in America, while recognizing the brave souls who have chosen to lend support and bring about positive change. Sergeant Woodard's story gives the young reader a glimpse of history, hope and faith in humanity.

Laura M. Williams

Laura M. Williams is a graduate of Marymount Manhattan College and Liberty University. She is a writer of children's books and a screenwriter focused on the tale of an American hero's contribution to the Civil Rights Movement.

As a direct descendant of Sergeant Isaac Woodard Jr., Laura recognizes the importance of preserving her uncle's compelling story and legacy. Her long-standing career in corporate investigation has proven effective to uncover the truth and tell an authentic story.

Victor Tavares

It is an honor to illustrate the story of Sergeant Woodard. It reminds us how evil thoughts turn into real violence.

There is more pain in suffering injustices than satisfaction in committing them. After experiencing both ways human kind created Constitutions. This is what keeps civilization from becoming barbaric.

We'll never live in a perfect State but the efforts of coming close to it will make our lives better.

Website : TheBlindingofIsaacWoodard.com

Twitter: @TheBlindingofIsaacWoodard

Instagram: TheBlindingofIsaacWoodard

Facebook: The Blinding of Isaac Woodard

Email: TheBlindingofIsaacWoodard@gmail.com

Booking and Speaking engagements Contact: L. Michelle (856) 295-1665

www.ingramcontent.com/pod-product-compliance
Lightning Source LLC
Chambersburg PA
CBHW041109210426

43209CB00063BA/1862